You Are Beautiful

Inspirational Stories for Girls about Happiness, Confidence and Self-Determination | Present for Girls

Amy Kissinger

THE BOOK BELONGS TO

....

....

CONTENTS

ALL THE WAYS I AM STRONG

I have always wondered how I can be strong. Should I lift lots of heavy bricks? Should I climb a massive mountain? Should I win every game of tug-of-war? My arms are so small and my hands are too. But I can still be strong, in my own special way.

Sometimes, I help my neighbour cross the road. She is old and slow, but she's still stronger than anyone that I know. She bakes lots of cookies and makes lots of fun. She tells me all the time that showing kindness is my biggest strength of all. I feed her cat every Monday and water her plants every Tuesday. I am strong enough to lift the watering can, but nothing is stronger than my mind.

I like to make my friends laugh when we take the bus to school. My best friend has pretty hair and her eyes are greener than grass. I tell her jokes for hours and hours to help the time to pass. I'm good at spelling and my friend is good at numbers, so we can always help each other. Friendship is a magical power, and it makes me feel stronger every day.

My parents get tired a lot because they work very difficult jobs. I like to clean my room and walk the dog because they do a lot for me. Mummy makes my favourite spaghetti every year on my birthday. Daddy always helps me with my homework and my chores. I love being helpful and it makes me feel strong when they smile. It always makes me smile, too.

There is a pretty bird that always flies into our garden. It has blue feathers on its wings and a long beak. I run outside every time that I hear it singing its beautiful songs. One day, the pretty bird fell out of the apple tree because it had hurt its wing. I picked it up from the grass and got a bandage to make it better again. Mummy took it to the vet and now the bird can fly again. It lands outside my window every morning and sings a special song just for me. It makes me feel so strong and special that I could almost fly as well.

When the weather gets cold outside, I always wear my hat and my scarf and my gloves. They are very precious to me because my grandmother knitted them. One day, I was walking through the town and I saw another little girl with very cold hands. They were red and shaky. She had no pockets to put them in.

"Are your hands cold?" I asked.

"They're very cold," she said. "I have no gloves".

"You can have mine," I told her, taking them off. "My gloves will match your pink coat!"

"That's very kind," the other girl replied. "Now my hands are warm and my heart feels warm inside".

I saw her again, a week later. She waved at me. Her fingers were knitted and pink. I was so happy that my gloves were keeping her hands warm. I knew that she would be extra strong when she was wearing those gloves because they were made with the power of love.

Last night, my older brother was very stressed because he had a school exam. His books were so big! He had so much to learn. I wanted to help, so I made him some tea. There was only one biscuit left in the tin, so I gave it to him. It made him smile. He was so happy that he broke the biscuit in half and gave one half to me. It tasted even better because we had shared it.

My lessons at school are a lot easier and much more fun. We get to paint colourful pictures every day. I love to paint pictures of all the things that I love. Last week, we had to paint a picture called 'All the Ways I Am Strong'. I painted myself as a superhero, wearing my hat and my scarf.

By my side, I painted the other girl who wears my gloves. I painted my best friend with her eyes greener than grass. I painted my brother with a tall pile of books and my parents drinking their favourite tea. I painted the old lady who lives next door with her cat. Then, I painted the bird with the blue feathers and the long beak flying above us.

I painted all those things because they are all the ways that I am strong. Whenever I am kind, helpful, funny, and thoughtful, I get stronger and stronger. Soon I will be so strong that I can lift a house all by myself. Maybe I can be a weightlifter and carry more weight than anybody else. I want to use my strength to make more people happy. The best show of strength in the world is to show love because everybody should feel love.

Do you imagine love to be big or small? Do you think it is a colour? I think that love is lots of colours. It is the colour of my best friend's green eyes and the colour of my knitted pink hat and scarf and gloves. It is also the colour of my neighbour's cat and the colour of my brother's hair. It is Mummy's favourite colour and Daddy's favourite colour too. It is blue like the wings of the pretty bird and orange like a sunset. It makes me feel warm and safe. It's something that I want to feel every day!

You can be kind, helpful, funny, and thoughtful too. What are all the ways that you are strong? Do you make your friends laugh? Do you help your neighbours? Do you look after animals? Do you see the magic in kindness and love? Once you find all the things that make you strong, you'll feel like you can lift a house as well!

THE GIRL WHO SAVES THE WORLD

I save the world every single day, but nobody knows. I have fought monsters and aliens and so many crazy things. When everybody else goes to sleep, I put on my superhero suit and fly higher than all the stars in the sky. I make sure that everybody is safe because sometimes the world can be a scary place. Sometimes people get stuck up trees. Sometimes they fall into the water. Sometimes they get lost on their way home.

I am always there to help them and they call me a hero. I save them from up the trees and from in the water and from the dark. My best adventures are the adventures when I get to help somebody else. I want the world to be a safe place. The world is always safer with heroes around. Sometimes, that special hero can be you.

I learned to fly when I was very young. I was running around the garden, then I started to float. I thought that I would float right up to the moon! I would have to live up there by myself and look down on the Earth. I wondered if the moon was really made of cheese.

But then I started to float back down. When I landed, I wanted to fly again. I scrunched my eyes shut and thought really hard about soaring all the way up into the sky. My feet felt tingly and so did my arms. I thought that wings might grow out of my back. But I didn't need wings. I could fly all by myself.

I love fashion very much. I decided to design my own superhero suit. It was blue and had a red mask and red cape. Whenever I fly, the cape flaps behind me. It makes me feel like I do have wings.

The first time I wore my superhero suit, I flew right out of the city and all over the countryside. I saw so many plants and animals. There was a baby bunny stuck under some branches. I swooped down and rescued it. When I brought the baby bunny back to its burrow, the mother rabbit thanked me.

I decided that I wanted to be a real superhero and help people too. The next time I flew out in my cape, I saw a little boy lost in the street. He was crying because he couldn't find his Mummy. I helped him go back the way he had walked. His Mummy was waiting for him. They didn't know who I was because of the mask. But I didn't need recognition. I had helped someone, and that made me feel good.

"Why are you always so sleepy?" My best friend asked one day.

"I had something important to do last night," I told her.

I have never told anyone that I'm a superhero. My adventures get crazier every night. Sometimes I fight the biggest monsters, or aliens from space. I save the world in secret. Nobody else believes in monsters or aliens. I know that they are real. But I don't fight them and save the world for credit. I do it because I love the world.

My favourite adventures are when I save people, or just help them. I have helped lots of old ladies and men across the road. I have carried shopping bags for people who had too many. I have stopped cars so that children could get to school. I pick up money that strangers have dropped on the floor. I fix power cuts so that people can have light. I have brought warm blankets to people who have forgotten their coats at home.

They always thank me and call me a hero. Some of them ask me to take my mask off so that they can thank me properly. I never take my mask off. I like keeping my identity a secret. But I do have a superhero name.

People call me the Super Strong Girl.

I feel strong and powerful every time I go on an adventure. One of the aliens that I fought had eight arms, like an octopus. I wrestled every single arm and won the fight. I never felt stronger than that until I saw my best friend in danger one day. That's when I knew that courage was the most important type of strength.

Lily is my best friend's name. When I saw her in danger, I recognised her bright orange hair. She was in a small boat on the river. Her family were in another boat. She was using a paddle to move about. I smiled while I watched her, until the sky got dark. There was lots of wind and rain and it pushed Lily's boat around. She dropped her paddle into the water. Then, her boat got blown right down the river. She was screaming.

I swooped down and followed the boat. The wind was swinging me around, but I never looked away from Lily. I followed her all the way down the river. She saw me and started calling to me.

"Super Strong Girl, help me!"

I flew as fast as I could. My cape blew around and covered my eyes, but I swept it away. Lily's boat got faster and faster. Her orange hair looked so dark because of the rain. I was worried that her boat would tip over! I had to save her before it was too late.

I got really close to the boat and reached out to Lily.

"Do you trust me?" I yelled.

"Yes!" She yelled back.

I grabbed her and started to fly up again. Below us, her boat tipped over. Lily clung onto me and I flew back the other way. The wind and rain started to get slower. Lily's family were sheltering under some trees. They waved to us. Her brothers started cheering.

"Super Strong Girl saved her!"

I flew down to the ground and put Lily down. She threw her arms around me in a hug. She told me all about it the next day at school. I could have told her that I was Super Strong Girl, but I didn't. I was happy that I saved Lily. I didn't need everyone to cheer for me. I knew that I could be courageous and strong as myself, not just as a superhero. That was what mattered.

THE FAIREST PRINCESS

I went to bed last night and I felt very strange. I was tingling all over, as if someone had sprinkled magic onto me. When I woke up, my bed was bigger and the sheets were softer. I looked out of the window and almost fell over in shock. I was high up in a castle and there was a whole kingdom just outside! There were so many little houses and lots of fields of flowers. It was the sunniest day that I had ever seen. Had I become a queen?

Inside the room, I found a tiara. I was not a queen, but I was a princess. When I opened the wardrobe, I found so many beautiful gowns. There was a pink gown, a blue gown, a yellow gown, and a purple gown. Yellow is my favourite colour, so I put on the yellow gown. With the tiara on my head, I felt ready to be a proper princess!

I was a bit scared to rule because it is so much responsibility. What if I made a mistake? What if I didn't know the answer to a question? What if I couldn't help all the people in the kingdom? But I wouldn't know until I tried, and every princess has to try. Cinderella had to be brave enough to go to the ball, Snow White had to be brave enough to run away and Sleeping Beauty had to be brave enough to fight against her curse.

I wanted to be a brave princess too. But I also wanted to be fair and kind. I loved to pretend to be a princess and rule over all my stuffed animals. My stuffed tiger was my butler, my stuffed elephant was my maid and my stuffed rhino was my chef. I was kind to all of them and they were very kind to me. I wondered if I would meet my stuffed animals in this palace too.

When I left the bedroom, everything I saw was magic! The walls were all golden and the floors were made of diamonds. There were huge paintings on the walls. Everything looked so wonderful and I was the princess of this palace. Maybe I could do some magic too. If I could,

I'd make all the land colourful and happy and fun. There would never be any rain here, only sunshine. All the animals would smile and dance. We'd all be as happy as could be.

"You're awake!" I heard someone call.

"Good morning," I replied.

"You've got so much to do today," the lady said.

"Because I'm the princess?"

"Of course!"

"What do I need to do first?"

"There is a competition and you need to choose a winner".

When I went outside, I found lots of magical creatures there. They were taking part in the competition. They all had to create some joy and I had to decide the winner. There was a fairy who shot fireworks out of her hands. Then, a dragon breathed fire in so many pretty shapes. A Pegasus flew across the top of a rainbow, then a good witch made all our wishes come true.

I couldn't pick a winner because all of them made me so happy. I decided that they could all be winners instead. All the creatures jumped for joy. The rainbow stayed in the sky all day.

After the competition, I went indoors for lunch. There was a table covered in food, but all the chairs were empty. I turned to the butler.

"Can't we invite some guests?"

"Who would you like to invite?" He asked.

"Everyone in the kingdom!"

The good witch cast another spell and the room grew ten sizes bigger! All the people and creatures in the kingdom could fit inside the room. There was so much food for all of us to eat. There was even some left over after everyone was full. I was delighted. We could have another party for dinner!

After lunch, I had to look at some new rules. Princesses always have to make choices. I wanted my choices to help all the people and creatures in my kingdom. The rules were all about being happy and having fun. The more fun that we could have, the better the kingdom would be.

At the end of the day, there was a huge dance. I was wearing the prettiest dress that had ever existed. It was pink and white and so sparkly. The dress felt like it went on for miles behind me. I wanted to dance for hours and hours. I knew that Mummy and Daddy would never have let me stay up so late. I was going to dance the night away. I was the princess. One of my rules was no bedtime!

The dance was my favourite part of the day. I got to see everyone happy and smiling. They did so many dances. First, we danced fast. I spun around so many times. Then, we danced slowly. I felt like a ballerina in a very long tutu. Sometimes I danced with my friends, but I danced a lot on my own.

Lots of people came to tell me how much they loved the dance. Seeing how I had made all of them so happy by being the princess made me happy too. I knew that I had been the fairest princess in all the land. Maybe I could be a queen someday.

I went to bed. I was still wearing my pretty dress because I was so tired. When I woke up, I was back in my bedroom at home. My feet hurt from all the dancing, and I still had the tiara on my head! Maybe I wasn't a princess now, but I was still fair and kind.

I think that we can all be princesses, if we act like princesses do. We can be brave and thoughtful. We are special too. Our strength is in our kindness and all the things that we do.

FACING A STORM

I've always been scared of storms. They're so big and loud, and they're strong enough to knock down trees. Last year, there was a storm so big that it broke one of the windows upstairs. The wind and the rain were dancing outside for hours. Sometimes, I think that storms might sweep me away. I feel so small when I see it start to rain. Then, the wind blows so hard that I think the house might blow right off the ground.

When the storms get really bad, Mummy and Daddy close all the curtains. We hide in the living room together under lots of blankets. Mummy makes the warmest hot chocolate and Daddy plays music to cover the sound of the rain. The storms usually don't last for very long. But once, there was a storm that lasted for a whole week! Every time I went outside, my hair and clothes got very wet. The wind was so strong that I could see lots of things flying through the air. I could hear the storm every night when I went to bed.

I wanted to be taller, so that I could catch the trees that fell over. I wanted to be heavier, so that the wind couldn't move me. I wanted to be stronger, so that I could fight all the raindrops by myself.

"How do I get stronger?" I asked my older brother one day.

His name is Ben. He's the strongest person that I know.

"You are already very strong," Ben told me.

"But I'm so little!"

"You are little, Maddie, but you are still strong. One day, you'll realise that you don't need to be big and tough to be strong".

Just after I turned seven, I got a pet dog. His name is Snowball. I called him that because he's small and fluffy and white, just like a snowball. I love to play with Snowball every day. We run outside together. He loves to play fetch with his favourite tennis ball. Every time I throw it, the ball bounces on and on and on. Snowball only has small legs, but he always catches the ball. When he brings it back, I throw it again.

Snowball loves to get cleaned too. I put him in the bath and wash his fluffy fur with soap and water. I'm always careful never to get soap in his eyes. When I rub him dry with a towel, his fur becomes even fluffier. He looks like an even bigger snowball.

Whenever there are storms now, I cuddle up close to Snowball. He is soft and warm. The storms outside are hard and cold. When I cuddle close to Snowball, I can forget about the storm outside. I can barely hear the rain and the wind. Snowball's breathing is gentle, but it is enough to distract me.

I always walk home from school with Ben. Sometimes, he brings Snowball too, but most times it is just us. We were walking home from school today when another storm started to hit. The wind got faster and the rain started to fall. I put the hood up on my yellow raincoat, but the rain started to soak me through. Ben grabbed my hand and we were running.

When we got to the house, the wind was pushing us towards the door. Ben opened it and we almost flew inside. I never knew that the wind could be so powerful! I ran through the house. I was looking for Snowball. He always barked when I got home, but I think the storms scared him. Sometimes he would hide under the blankets all day. One time, it took me an hour to find him.

"I can't find Snowball!" I called to Ben.

"He must be in here somewhere," Ben said.

I ran back into the kitchen and looked out of the window. I could see something small moving around. It looked like something white and fluffy. It was Snowball! He was hiding under the bushes from the storm. I had to bring him inside. I had to make sure that he was safe.

I put my yellow hood back up and ran out of the door. The wind was pushing me and the rain was hitting me in the face. I called out to Snowball, but he stayed hiding. The grass was so wet that I almost slipped. I wanted to run back inside, but I had to rescue Snowball from the storm.

"I'm coming, Snowball!" I shouted.

The wind and rain were so loud. I think it might have been one of the biggest storms ever! I kept pushing on, trying to be stronger than the wind. I finally got to Snowball. He jumped into my arms, his fluffy fur all long and wet. I held him tightly as I ran back to the house. We almost got blown over, but I pushed back against the wind. We flew through the door and I slammed it shut.

"Where did you go?" Ben asked.

"Snowball was out in the garden, I had to rescue him".

"Going out into the storm could have been dangerous, Maddie".

"I had to be brave," I told Ben. "Otherwise, Snowball could have been blown away".

"I told you that you didn't need to be big to be strong," Ben smiled.

I think that he's right. I am little, but I am strong. I am brave when I need to be brave. I can be as powerful as a storm. Even when the wind tried to blow me away, I didn't let it. I saved Snowball and got us both out of the storm. Now I know that I don't need to be scared of storms because I can make them small when I find the strength to feel big. I don't need to be big, as long as I feel big.

Nothing is as big or strong as a powerful girl. I know that I can be that powerful girl every single day.

WHEN I BECAME FAMOUS

I never believed in witches. But when I met Emerald, I changed my mind. She was a good witch and she only cast good spells. I always walked past her on my way to school and I always waved to her. One day, I thought she looked hungry, so I offered her my sandwich.

"You are a very kind girl, Poppy," she said. "I will grant you a wish".

I didn't know what to wish for. There were so many wonderful things that I dreamed about. One special game that I always played with my friends was a game about being famous. We would pretend to be famous and act out all the things we would do. Katie wanted to be a rock star, Lola wanted to be a politician and Rebecca wanted to be a ballerina. I never knew what I would do if I was famous.

"I want to be famous for a day," I told Emerald.

She cast a spell and told me that my wish had come true. I kept on walking and then I saw cameras flashing across the street. People were calling my name and cheering!

"Amber! Over here, Amber!"

I was a bit scared because they were so loud. But they didn't get too close to me. They started taking pictures with their cameras. I wondered if I would see them in magazines. I loved reading magazines about famous women and girls. They seemed so grown up. I always wanted to be just like them.

I wasn't sure what I was famous for. How could I find out? When I turned to look back down the road, Emerald had disappeared.

A black car pulled up in front of me. It was a limo! The door opened and my big sister, Elizabeth, jumped out. She grabbed my hand and pulled me into the limo. My Daddy was driving it! I wondered if the spell had made us all famous.

"Where are we going?" I asked Elizabeth.

"To the Diamond Hall," Elizabeth said.

The Diamond Hall was huge! It was a building where lots of famous people went. Katie wanted to become a rock star and have a concert in the Diamond Hall. Lola wanted to talk about politics there. Rebecca wanted to perform ballet on that stage. But what was I going to do in the Diamond Hall?

"Is it a special occasion?" I asked.

Elizabeth laughed. "It's for your speech!"

A speech? I was never confident enough to talk in public. I was always scared to answer questions in class at school. When I answered, I always kept my eyes down. How was I going to make a speech? One thousand people could fit inside the Diamond Hall. I would have to stand on the stage in front of them all!

When the limo got to the Diamond Hall, I could see crowds of people. They were all holding up banners with my name on them. They had all arrived just to see me. I didn't even know what my speech was about! I wished that I'd asked Emerald what I would be famous for.

I followed Elizabeth into the Diamond Hall. She told me to sit down at a desk. I was going to sign autographs for my fans. They came into the room one at a time. I asked for their names and then signed autographs for them. One girl looked like she was so happy to see me.

"I love your work," she told me.

"Thank you," I said. "What do you love the most?"

"I love everything about your writing," the girl responded.

So, I was a famous writer! I always loved to write. I had never told Emerald that I wrote stories, but she was a witch, so she must have known. I couldn't wait to thank her for granting my wish! She was so clever.

After the autographs, I followed Elizabeth and our parents backstage. I asked them if I had written my speech down on paper, but they told me that I never wrote my speeches down. I would just have to make it up myself on the stage.

Elizabeth sent me into a dressing room. There were two kind ladies who did my hair and makeup for me. When I looked in the mirror, I really did look famous. My whole face was sparkling. My straight hair had been made really curly. I looked like I could be in a film.

But even though I looked famous, I still couldn't feel confident. What if I made a fool of myself? All those people would laugh at me! Even if they liked my writing, they might hate my speaking. I didn't know what to do.

"You look scared," a voice said.

I turned around and saw Emerald. She must have cast a spell to transport herself into the room. I was happy to see her.

"I'm so nervous!" I told her. "I can't make a speech".

"You love to write," Emerald replied. "You don't always have to write on paper. You can write in your head too. You'll make a great speech".

"But what are all my books about?" I asked. "I know I'm a writer".

"You write a lot about gratitude and life lessons. People love to read them because they're so important. Think about all the things you are grateful for. Then you'll know what to say".

I thought about her words as I stepped onto the stage. I was shaking with nerves. I had a microphone in my hand. The Diamond Hall was full of people.

For a minute, I couldn't think of anything to say. But I remembered what Emerald had told me. I thought about how Mummy taught me to read and how Daddy taught me to write. If they hadn't, I would never have been able to start writing stories. I talked to the crowd about my gratitude. I was also grateful for Elizabeth. She was always an amazing big sister. She made me a better person.

When my speech was over, the room burst into applause. I could see Emerald stood at the side of the stage. Even though I knew she'd only made me famous for a day, I'd remember what she'd told me about gratitude. I would write more stories and one day maybe I could be a famous writer for real. And I'd remember everyone who had helped me along the way.

BELIEVING IN UNICORNS

I have always loved unicorns. They are my favourite animal because they're so magical. My dream has always been to find a unicorn and ride on it like a horse. We would run faster than light, all around the city. I could wear a pretty dress that was the same colour as my unicorn. Maybe it would have rainbow fur and a rainbow horn. I'd look like a princess riding on its back.

One day, Mummy told me that we were going on a special camping trip. It was in a green forest. I felt like I was in a fairytale. We were all staying in a huge tent. It was so big that I had my own room! There was enough space for seven people in the room. It would have been nice to have some friends with me, or a pet.

When we went walking in the forest, I was walking behind Mummy and Daddy. I ran off the path when I saw a pretty flower. It was gold and shiny. I wanted to touch it and see if it was real. But then I saw something much bigger and much more magical. It was a unicorn!

It had rainbow fur and a rainbow horn. Its body was strong and it shimmered in the sunlight. I couldn't speak. I never thought that I would get to meet a real unicorn! It was even more special than I had ever imagined.

"Are you real?" I asked.

The unicorn looked at me. "I am real," it replied.

I knew that unicorns were real, and I knew that they could talk! It was the most amazing day of my life.

"What's your name? My name is Lucy".

"My name is Stardust," the unicorn said.

"What a beautiful name!"

I could hear footsteps behind me. Mummy and Daddy were coming to look for me. When I looked back, Stardust had vanished. Maybe she didn't want anyone else to see her except me? I decided to keep the unicorn a secret. I hoped that I could see her again.

We had hot chocolate in the tent before bed. I brushed my teeth and put on my pyjamas and socks. Then, I slid into my sleeping bag. I had an extra blanket to keep me warm as well. It was the middle of the night when I had something in that room of the tent with me. There were hooves and I could make out the shape of a horse with a horn. It was the unicorn!

"I'm sorry that I ran away before," Stardust said.

"It's okay," I replied. "I kept you a secret".

Stardust smiled. "Thank you. I don't usually speak to humans".

"Why did you speak to me?"

"Unicorns can only exist if people believe in them. You believe in me, so I exist. I get my strength from your strength".

"But I'm not strong," I said. "My arms are very small and so are my legs. I can only lift very light things".

"Your body is not strong, but your imagination is. Having a strong imagination is one of the most important things in the world".

I couldn't believe it! Stardust existed because of my imagination. I always dreamed of a rainbow unicorn. I never thought that my dreams would make that unicorn real. I never thought that my imagination could be so strong. Daddy always told me that it was important to dream. I would keep dreaming of Stardust now that I'd met her.

"Would you like to go for a ride?" Stardust asked. "We could see all of the forest in one night".

I clapped my hands and jumped out of my sleeping bag. I hopped onto Stardust's back and she carried me out of the tent. When we got outside, she started to run. Her legs were so strong and she could run so fast. She galloped like a horse, but she was more magical. I almost thought that we were going to fly.

The forest really was magical! Everywhere Stardust took me, I could see things that I thought were only real in books. There were twenty pixies, all of them living in a tree. I saw fairies flying as high as the stars. There was even a cow with wings jumping over the moon, like in the nursery rhyme. The forest was enchanted by magic.

"Only you can see them," Stardust told me.

"What about Mummy and Daddy?" I asked her.

"They can't see these magical things because they don't have your imagination. Their dreams aren't as strong as yours".

"I must make them believe!" I cried.

I wanted Mummy and Daddy to be able to see this magical world with me. They thought that the forest was just trees and mud and leaves. The river just looked like water to them. But I could see that it was made out of glitter. There were mermaids swimming in it. The mermaids waved to me as Stardust ran past. I waved back at them all.

The forest was so huge, but I saw it all in one night. Every part was more magical than the last part. I wished that it would never end. But when Stardust took me back to the tent, I was almost falling asleep. I wanted to climb back into my sleeping bag.

When I woke up, I found Mummy and Daddy outside the tent. They were looking at the ground.

"There are hoof prints," Mummy said.

"It must have been a horse," Daddy said.

"It was a unicorn!" I told them.

"But unicorns aren't real," Mummy replied.

"Yes, they are! You just have to believe in them. If your imagination is strong enough, you will see them".

Mummy and Daddy both closed their eyes. They were concentrating. Then, I saw Stardust appear! I was thinking about her again. But there were two other unicorns with her. One unicorn was green, the other was yellow. Mummy's favourite colour was green and Daddy's favourite was yellow. They believed in the unicorns and made them exist!

Stardust nodded at me and then ran back into the forest. The other two unicorns followed her. Mummy and Daddy were delighted. I had helped them find their imaginations. Now there were two more unicorns in the world!

STORY 7:

THE DAY I RACED MY CAR

I've loved cars all my life. Some of them are big, some of them are small, some of them have fast wheels, and some of them are much slower. They come in all the colours of the rainbow: red and blue and yellow and green and all the colours in between. I always dreamed of getting into a car that was as sparkly as my favourite silver dress and speeding off so fast that all the people I passed looked like blurs.

Daddy always let me watch the car races with him. They all went so fast and never made any mistakes. The cars were smaller than any other cars that I'd seen. They were painted with bright colours and amazing patterns. I told Daddy that when I was older, I wanted to buy my own car and paint it. I would be the fastest racer and win every race that I entered. My tyres would never wear out. I'd be able to drive up to the stars!

"It takes a long time to become a race driver," Daddy said.

I knew that I could do it in no time at all.

There are no little girl race car drivers that I know. I made my own race car out of a cardboard box and raced it around the garden. All the birds flew behind me. They flapped their wings as hard as they could, but my race car was faster. I painted pretty patterns all over the sides. I even painted the wheels the brightest shade of blue.

One day, I went to sleep and dreamed that I was winning an amazing race. I was driving faster than all the other racers. My bright blue wheels were spinning, and I was turning every corner. Just as I was about to reach the finish line, I woke up. But when I opened my eyes, I wasn't in my bed at home.

I was sitting in a real race car with real blue wheels and a really fast engine. When I looked around, I saw lots of other little girls sitting in race cars too. They were all painted with beautiful colours, especially on the wheels. But I knew that I could race faster than all of them. My blue wheels were so shiny that they looked like stars.

"Where am I?" I asked the girl next to me.

"We're about to race," she said. "I think I'm going to win".

I never thought that my racing dream would come true so quickly. But when I heard the starting sound, I started to drive faster than I ever imagined. I zoomed ahead of all the other girls. I almost felt as though the wheels had left the ground and I was driving on air. I completed my first two laps in under a minute.

The racecourse had many twists and turns. My hands were like magic on the steering wheel. I never thought that I had enough strength to move so quickly, but I was moving faster than light. The entire racecourse was surrounded by the tallest trees. We were racing inside the most magical forest. I even thought that I could see fairies high up in the trees.

The fairies must have granted my wish!

I was surrounded by lots of other girls who were all special race car drivers too. Their cars were fast, but none of them were quite as fast as me. I think that my shiny blue wheels were enchanted with magic. The fairies must have heard me wishing that I could win a race too!

I had to finish ten laps in the first position to win the race. After I started my ninth lap, I was sure that I would win. The girl who had told me about the race at the start was just behind me. Her car was coming closer and closer. Just as she was about to overtake me, her car flew off towards the side of the racecourse and crashed into some trees.

I could have kept on driving and won the race, but I stopped immediately. I jumped out of my race car and ran over to her. She was trying to get out of her own car.

"I'll help you!" I cried.

"Now my car is ruined," she replied. "I won't be able to finish the race!"

All the other drivers had flown past us, making their way towards the finish line. I tried to help her push her car free, but it was stuck between the trees. One of her bright pink wheels had fallen off and rolled away.

The other girl looked like she was about to cry. I could have run back to my car, but that would have been very unkind, and I wanted to cheer her up. I knew how badly she wanted to finish the race.

"We'll finish the race together," I told her. "We can drive together in my car".

"But you could have won," she said. "Why did you stop?"

"Because you needed help," I replied. "And helping somebody in need is always more important".

"My name is Cleo," the other girl told me. "What's yours?"

"I'm Sophie," I replied. "And I think that in my car with its fast blue wheels, we could still win the race".

"We'll have to drive faster than ever!"

We both climbed into my race car and held the steering wheel together. The race car started to drive, faster than it ever had before. The other racers were already getting close to the finish line, but we didn't lose hope. Cleo pulled the steering wheel and I pushed the pedals. Together, we started to overtake the other racers.

The finish line was just in sight. We crossed it before anyone else! We got to stand together and share the trophy. Being able to share the victory and make somebody else happy made winning the race feel even better than I imagined. The fairies flew above our heads, sprinkling us with magic.

When I woke up the next morning, I looked outside my window. My special race car with the bright blue wheels was just outside! I went out to see if it was real or another dream. Then, I jumped into the race car and sped off, laughing all the way.

STORY 8:

HOW I HELPED A FRIEND

Everyone has secrets. I have secrets and so do you. We all have things that we want to keep to ourselves. But what if there was a secret that could hurt somebody else? Would you tell? Or would you pretend you knew nothing about it? I learned all about that the day that I discovered a secret myself.

Pearl is my best friend. We've been friends ever since we were babies. We used to talk to each other in baby language. Nobody else could ever understand except us. We grew up together. We go to school together. We do everything together. I tell her jokes and she draws pictures for me. She's very good at drawing.

One day, Pearl entered a competition and one of her drawings won! She got a special award. I was so happy for her. I thought of lots of jokes about art.

"What is red and smells like yellow paint? Red paint!"

"What do artists love to draw before they go to sleep? Their curtains!"

"What did the police say about the criminal artist? He was sketchy!"

"What happened when two artists had a football match? It ended in a draw!"

Pearl laughed at all my jokes. She wanted to enter more competitions with her art. Her best picture was a painting of three princesses. The first princess had black hair and she was holding a microphone. The second princess had red hair and she was writing at a desk. The third princess had green hair and she was playing the trumpet. It was a magical picture. Pearl said that it was inspired by how amazing girls are and how they can do anything they set their minds to.

I discovered a secret that Pearl didn't know when I was sat in my art class at school. I was sat next to my other friend, Susie. She was telling me that one of her paintings had been put on the wall of the classroom. I was excited for her. But when I saw the painting, I knew that Susie didn't paint it. It was Pearl's painting of the three princesses! Susie must have found it and pretended it was hers.

"That's Pearl's painting," I said.

"No, I painted it," Susie replied.

"I know that Pearl painted it," I insisted. "Lying about your work is wrong".

"Please don't tell anyone," Susie said.

I didn't know what to do. Susie was my friend, but Pearl was my friend too. And I knew that lying was wrong. But pretending that someone else's work is yours was even more wrong. But if I told Pearl, she would be angry with Susie. And Susie would be angry with me. I didn't want anyone to be angry. But I didn't want Susie to get credit for Pearl's work, either.

I asked my sister, Marie, about it when I got home. She listened while I told her everything.

"I think you should tell Pearl," Marie said.

"But then she'll be mad at Susie," I replied. "And Susie will get into trouble".

"Susie shouldn't have taken the painting," Marie told me. "If she gets into trouble, it will help her learn. You should do the right thing, May".

I thought about what Marie said. I knew that she was right. Susie would probably get into trouble, but she wouldn't do it again. And Pearl would thank me. Taking credit for someone else's work was always wrong. Maybe if Susie said sorry, Pearl would still be her friend. And Susie might not be mad at me as well.

The next day, I told Pearl about the painting. She was upset that Susie took her painting and pretended that it was hers. Together, we went to see the art teacher. She gave the painting back to Pearl and said that she would talk to Susie. Pearl was happy to have her painting back. I knew that I'd done the right thing by telling Susie's secret. But I still felt sad that Susie would get into trouble.

We saw Susie on the bus after school. She looked sad and she didn't want to talk to me at first. But when the bus started moving, Susie came and sat next to us. She wanted to apologise to Pearl.

"I'm sorry for taking your painting," she said. "I shouldn't have done it. I hope we can still be friends".

"I'm glad that you know it was wrong," Pearl replied. "I still want to be friends".

"I promise I'll never take your paintings again," Susie told her.

"I'm glad you're still friends," I said.

"I'm sorry that I told you to lie, May," Susie said to me. "It was wrong".

"I feel better because I told the truth," I responded. "And I still want to be friends as well. But no more bad secrets".

We all agreed to be friends and never keep secrets from each other. On the weekend, we went to the park together. We decided to dress as the three princesses. We played lots of games and danced around together for hours. Being friends felt so much better than not being friends. And being friends without secrets was the best.

I told Marie what happened. She said that she was proud of me.

"It takes courage to tell a secret," she said. "Being brave can be scary, but it feels better than lying".

She was right. If I had kept Susie's secret, we might never have been friends again. Pearl might have hated me. But we all made up instead. Pearl got to display her painting as her own work. Susie and I told her that it was amazing. She decided to enter it into a competition. Pearl named the painting 'Three Best Friends'. It is still my favourite painting that she has ever painted.

THE GIRL NEXT DOOR

There's a girl next door called Sadie. I always thought that Sadie was very strange. She is so quiet and I barely ever see her face when she passes by our house. She hides her face under her long blonde hair. One of my friends said that Sadie is strange because she has no confidence. I think that's why Sadie doesn't talk to people very much.

Yesterday, I told Grandma about Sadie. I told her that I thought Sadie was odd.

"Why do you think that?" Grandma asked.

"Because she's so quiet and shy," I said.

"It's not very kind to call people odd," Grandma told me. "You don't know what Sadie is really like".

I went to bed thinking about what she said. When I woke up this morning, I was in a different bed! My hair wasn't dark anymore, it was blonde. My pink bedsheets were purple instead. There were beautiful paintings on the walls. They were paintings of flowers and butterflies and angels. I wished that I could paint as well as that.

I got out of bed and ran to the mirror. But it wasn't me who was looking back. It was Sadie! I waved my hand and she waved hers too. I hopped on one foot and she hopped too. I shook my hair and she shook hers too. I'd turned into Sadie overnight!

I was wearing yellow pyjamas and they were really soft. Sadie had a lot more paintings on her desk. She had painted all the things she could see out of her window. There were paintings of people passing by and driving in their cars. There was one of a girl with dark hair skipping along the pavement. The girl was wearing red and green dungarees. It was me! Sadie painted me so well.

"Sadie, are you ready for school?" Somebody called from downstairs.

It was Sadie's Mummy! How was I going to explain this to her? And was Sadie in my body?

I would have to pretend until I knew for sure. Maybe I could catch Sadie in my body before school.

"I'm getting dressed!" I called back.

I opened the wardrobe and pulled out Sadie's school uniform. I ran to wash my hands and face in the bathroom before I put it on. The school uniform fit perfectly. I was about to braid my hair, but then I remembered how Sadie always wore her hair. She wore it long and blonde, and it looked beautiful.

When I went downstairs, Sadie's Mummy made breakfast. She started to talk to me about this interesting book that Sadie was reading. I wasn't sure what to say because I hadn't read the book. But I always saw Sadie reading wherever she went. Her hair looked even longer when she was leaning over a book.

I left the house at half past eight to get on the school bus. I could see another girl waiting down the road at the bus stop. It was me! My dark hair was braided, but not very well. Sadie must have realised what happened and tried to pretend to be me. I ran towards her.

"Sadie, is that you?"

"Olivia, you're me!" Sadie exclaimed.

"Something must have happened to make us change bodies," I said.

"I think we'll change back tonight," Sadie told me. "We can't be stuck forever".

"We have to pretend until then," I replied.

I looked at her hair again and told her to wear it down. I always braided my hair. But it looked really nice when Sadie took it out of her bad braid. We looked a bit like sisters, one with blonde hair and one with dark hair.

Sadie was so nice when she spoke to me at the bus stop. I had always called her strange and I felt very ashamed of myself. I never stopped to talk to her. I laughed behind her back because I thought she was odd. Grandma was right. I had been mean about Sadie and I regretted it.

On the bus, we talked some more. Sadie told me about her book. It was about an artist who was famous for painting angels. I loved listening. I decided to read the book myself when I was back in my body.

When we got to school, I noticed people pointing at me and giggling. I remembered that I was in Sadie's body. Somebody pointed at me and called me a mean name. I wanted to shout at them to leave Sadie alone, but then I remembered that I was pretending to be Sadie. In my body, Sadie ran past. I followed after her.

All the teachers were so nice to me in my lessons. Sadie was super smart. She was smarter than anyone else in the class. The teachers all loved Sadie because they knew that she was kind and clever. I was ashamed of myself again for not noticing her properly. I planned to apologise and ask her if she wanted to be friends.

When we went for our lunch, another girl called out my name.

"Olivia, what are you doing with that weird girl?"

"What should I say?" Sadie whispered.

"Tell her why she shouldn't be so mean," I told her.

Sadie, pretending to be me, turned to the other girl. "Don't call people weird. It's unkind and it upsets people. Just because someone is different doesn't make them weird".

The other girl hung her head and looked ashamed. I linked arms with Sadie and we skipped down to the lunch queue. Everybody was looking at me in Sadie's body more nicely. Two people even came over and apologised for calling

Sadie names. Sadie whispered to me to pretend to be her and tell them it was okay. Sadie was so forgiving and kind. She gave everyone a second chance.

"I'm so sorry for ignoring you before," I told Sadie on our way home. "I hope you can forgive me".

Sadie flung her arms around me and hugged me! It felt odd to be hugged by myself, but I hugged back. Sadie and I made a pinky promise to be friends forever. When I went to sleep in Sadie's yellow pyjamas that night, I smiled.

When I woke up, I was myself again!

I looked out of the window and saw Sadie outside in her garden. She waved to me and I waved back. I know that I'll never talk about someone behind their back again. I'll tell Grandma that she was right. Being kind makes me feel much nicer than being mean. Kindness is the strength I never knew I had before.

HOW I FOUND HAPPINESS

I always wonder what happiness looks like. I wonder if it has a special colour or a special sound. Happiness feels warm and fuzzy to me. It makes me smile even on the rainiest days. It helps me to spend time with my family and my friends. It is like a cloud of candyfloss floating over a sea of lemonade. In my happy world, all the flowers are lollipops and all the trees are chocolate.

But the day that I found happiness was the best day of all. I kept on finding it over and over again. It was in all the places that I least expected. Then it jumped out at me like a friendly bunny. My smile got bigger and bigger. I thought that it would get too big for my small face.

I first found happiness when I woke up. I had fallen asleep on the sofa the night before. Daddy had carried me upstairs and tucked me into bed. He was so kind that he didn't wake me up. He made sure I was comfortable with all my stuffed animals around me. Then, I found happiness again when I went downstairs. My older brother, Steven, was sitting at the table. He was eating breakfast.

"Why aren't you eating the chocolate cereal?" I asked.

"There was only a little left," he replied. "I saved it for you".

I loved the chocolate cereal, but Steven loved it even more than me. He could have eaten it, but he was thoughtful enough to share. His kind act made me smile and I promised to return it soon. I also helped him find his shoes before school because he'd lost them. Then, he walked with me to the school gates and said goodbye.

I skipped into school and met my three best friends. I told Lizzie that I liked her hairstyle. I laughed at all of Sofia's jokes. I started to learn a new dance routine that Melissa had made up. I made them all smile. They made me smile too. I think that happiness is also friendship in disguise. It's impossible to be sad when you've got such amazing best friends to make you grin!

I stumbled a little in my lessons that day. I was good at numbers, but I wasn't as good at spelling. I got confused over lots of the big words. My teacher, Miss Matthews, stopped by my desk when she was walking around the room. I have always liked Miss Matthews very much. She is nice to everyone, even the students who misbehave.

"Are you stuck?" She asked.

"I am," I said. "I don't know how to spell any of these words!"

She sat down next to me and helped me to spell each word. She even sounded them out for me so that I understood. I wrote all the words out by myself and spelled them perfectly. All I needed was a little help. If Miss Matthews wasn't so caring, she wouldn't have helped me. Her kindness filled me with even more happiness.

At lunchtime, I got to create happiness myself. I had found happiness so many times already that day, now I got to help somebody else find it. Lizzie had forgotten her lunch at home. She was sad because she was really hungry. I gave her two of my sandwiches and my apple. Apples were my favourite, but I wanted her to have it because she needed it more. Sofia and Melissa gave her some of their lunch too. It felt like we were all having an indoor picnic!

After school, I walked home by myself. I saw a cat on the way. It was trying to squeeze through a gate, but it was stuck. The cat saw me and it meowed in panic. I think it was asking me to help it. I'd always been a bit scared of cats because they are so quick. But this cat needed my help. I got closer and helped the cat to squeeze through where it was stuck. The cat meowed again and let me pat its head.

As soon as I opened the front door, Mummy ran towards me.

"Something amazing has happened!"

"What is it?" I asked.

"Grandma is home from the hospital," she told me.

I jumped for joy! Grandma had been in the hospital for weeks. I had been really worried about her. But now, she was back at home where she belonged. I didn't think it was possible to ever be happier. I decided to make some cookies to bring to her. I wanted them to be shaped like all the things that remind me of happiness.

I made a cookie of the sun and a cookie of the moon. I made cookies shaped like all my family. I made three cookies shaped like my best friends. I made a cookie that looked like Miss Matthews. I made one shaped like the cat I saw.

I iced words onto them too:

- STRENGTH

- LOVE

- COURAGE

- KINDNESS

- FRIENDSHIP

Seeing all of those things made me realise that happiness isn't one big thing. It is lots of small things. All the small things add up like the most wonderful sum. When you put so many small signs of happiness together, it spreads even faster around everyone that you know. Kindness leads to happiness, strength leads to happiness and thoughtfulness leads to happiness.

Wherever you are and whatever you do, you'll always be able to find happiness. You just need to look for all the little things. Even if it is very small, happiness will still find you. And you can always find happiness too.

DISCLAIMER

This book contains opinions and ideas of the author and is meant to teach the reader informative and helpful knowledge while due care should be taken by the user in the application of the information provided. The instructions and strategies are possibly not right for every reader and there is no guarantee that they work for everyone. Using this book and implementing the information/recipes therein contained is explicitly your own responsibility and risk. This work with all its contents, does not guarantee correctness, completion, quality or correctness of the provided information. Misinformation or misprints cannot be completely eliminated.